The Secrets Of Making $10,000

On Ebay in 30 Days

By Omar Johnson

I0463685

This book is dedicated to those who are relentless in their pursuit of excellence.

Table of Contents

Introduction

Hello my name is Omar Johnson and welcome to "The Secrets of Making $10,000 on Ebay in 30 Days". Let me start of by saying I LOVE Ebay. Why? Because I am a very successful powerseller on Ebay who is generating a ton of cash on a daily consistent basis. Furthermore, Ebay enabled me to Fire MY Boss and quit my 9 to 5 job as a bean counter accountant.

Making money on Ebay literally changed my lifestyle. I'm not trying to impress you, I'm telling you this because I want you to have a clear picture of how your life will change financially when you become a successful seller on Ebay. In "The Secrets of Making $10,000 on Ebay in 30 Days" I reveal to you the exact map and blueprint that I use to make money and quite frankly you need a map and a blueprint if you also want to be a successful seller who makes money on Ebay. Would you ever attempt to sail a ship to a destination without a map and compass? Would you ever attempt to build a building without a blueprint? Of course not.

So why should you become a seller on Ebay? The answer is simple. Selling on Ebay offers numerous advantages to you.

1) It is a built in marketplace consisting of 180 million register users who are predominantly buyers.

2) There are over 18,000 categories for items.

3) Selling items on Ebay requires little or no capital at all when you use the principles of leverage.

4) You have an instant home business.

For those of you who are already Ebay sellers great! I still could teach you a trick or two with my system. For those of you who are beginners, here is my Ebay story. It will put you on the fast track to becoming a successful seller on Ebay. I am qualified to say this because as I mentioned previously I am an Ebay powerseller.

A powerseller is a distinction that Ebay places on its members who consistently rank among the successful sellers in terms of product sales and customer satisfaction.

My Ebay Story

My first encounter with Ebay occurred as a result of my desire of wanting to buy music equipment at discount prices. I was just plain tired of paying the full prices at the local Sam Ash Music Store. So I registered with Ebay as a buyer and began my quest for low price music equipment.

Registering as a buyer was pretty easy, all I had to do was give them my name, address, birth date, telephone number, e-mail address and accept the terms of the Ebay's user agreement, which I anxiously did barely reading it.

I was on my way. I immediately began bidding on three auctions for music equipment. Bidding on these auctions was quite intoxicating because of the whole idea of wanting something and having to compete with other bidders to get it. As a former athlete, this had my competitive juices flowing but not overflowing.

This was business and I had to keep my emotions in check. I did not want to overbid and overpay for an item. Obviously a seller thinks on the contrary, they want the bidders to get in a bidding war thereby driving up the price of the items resulting in maximum profits for them.

The three auctions ended and I only won one out of the three. In the other two auctions I was outbid in the final seconds. This is the norm on Ebay. There are a lot of veteran buyers out there and through practice they have acquired the skills necessary to win an auction at the last second. These last second bidders are unaffectionately referred to as snipers.

Super Tip: How to snipe an auction on Ebay. Open an auction that you wish to bid on in two separate browser windows. Log in to your account in the second browser window auction and enter the highest amount you are willing to pay for the item and click the continue button. When you click the continue button the next page that you will see is the review and confirm bid.

Do not click on the "confirm bid" button at the bottom of the page yet. Occasionally "reload" or refresh" the first browser window to keep track of the time remaining and the current price before the auction ends. When there is about 15 seconds left before the auction ends, click the "confirm bid" button in the second browser window. This is how you snipe an auction on Ebay.

The reason to why I am relating my experiences as a buyer is because you have to know the psychology of buying and the buyer to become a great seller. Selling is both an art and a science. It involves having an existing product or creating one, advertising and marketing the product to stimulate demand for it (which is basically the consumer feeling that they either want or need the product), affixing a price to the product that the market could both bear and the seller could make a profit, and finally making the sale. Actually I shouldn't say finally, because you want to keep selling to the same customers over and over again, establishing a customer base as well as a foundation for your business.

Buying is based on want or need. After the basic necessities are satisfied involving shelter, clothing and food, people buy because they want things. For example, you need soap to take a shower or bath, it's a necessity at least I hope it is. However, you don't need a vanilla ice cream you just simply want one. So when you see an ice cream stand on the street, you start to feel an urge to have an ice cream, so you buy it "can I have a vanilla ice cream with a sugar cone and sprinkles on top". People buy based on impulse.

I continued to buy music equipment as well as other things on Ebay. Items that I really want and feel that I am getting a good price for I simply "buy it now ".

I like this feature that Ebay offers its' sellers, because it allows the sellers to establish a price that they are willing to sell an item for immediately before any bids have taken place. Once the first bid is entered the "buy it now " feature is removed, unless it's a fixed price auction. (we will cover this later)

I see an auction for a brand name, used, in mint condition microphone, that normally cost $600 new, selling for $350 if you "buy it now". After reading the description of the item and feeling satisfied that it met my standards. I "buy it now" for the $350. My buying escapades continue for a couple of weeks.

As a buyer, I always paid for the item as soon as the auction ended and of course the various sellers highly appreciated that and let the Ebay community know by leaving me positive feedback for each and every one of the transactions I won.

For example, the seller of the auction for the microphone left the following comments. "fast payment smooth transaction I highly recommend this Ebayer". I in turn left positive feedback for them

Feedback

Feedback is essentially the lifeblood of Ebay. It is so to speak a report card on how you performed in a transaction as a seller or buyer. Other Ebay members usually determine if they want to buy from you based on your feedback rating. If your rating is high, it instills confidence in a buyer and chances are they will bid on the item you are selling. If it is low it would of course have the opposite effect. Ebay became the number one auction place in the world because of their feedback system. Whether they can maintain their number one position remains to be seen.

In May of 2008, Ebay changed its entire feedback system and in my opinion it gives the advantage totally to the buyer. Here's why. Prior to this drastic change to the Ebay system both buyers and sellers were allowed to leave positive, negative and neutral feedback. However, presently this is no longer the case. While buyers are still allowed to leave positive, negative and neutral feedback, sellers are only allowed to leave positive feedback for buyers.

This totally sucks because sellers are no longer able to express their opinion unless it's positive of how a transaction truly went with a buyer. Ebay has received a lot of flack from its' powerful community of sellers as a result of these ridiculous changes which also includes the implementation of a detail seller rating system (DSR) which allows buyers to anonymously leave detailed seller ratings in four areas. These areas are:

1) Item as described

2) Communication

3) Shipping time

4) Shipping and handling charges

The detailed seller rating system is based on a one to five star scale. Five stars is the highest rating and one star is the lowest. Although detail seller ratings are not included in the calculation of the seller's feedback score they still affect your ability to sell on Ebay. Here's how.

Ebay implemented a new algorithm to its search engine that weighs a seller's detail seller rating against the detail seller rating average scores of other sellers whom are selling items in the same category. If your detail seller rating is higher you will appear in a high position on Ebay's search results page. If it is low it will have the opposite effect.

Why is this so important to you as a seller? Because prior to these new changes Ebay's default search was designed to let every auction listing have an equal chance to appear at the top or near the top of the search results page because the default settings were set to show the auctions ending soonest. This is no longer the case. The new default settings are now set to Best Match. In the Best Match default settings system your position in the search results page is determined by numerous factors such as the price of your item, your shipping cost, how recently you have sold that same item and of course your detailed seller rating.

You must maintain a DSR minimum of 4.3

In addition to affecting where your auctions appear on Ebay's search engine, in order to continuing selling on Ebay you must maintain a minimum of 4.3 on all DSR's or you can no longer list items for sale on Ebay. You will be blocked. Will these changes backfire on Ebay?

To a certain extent it already has and they had to make some adjustments. If these stringent policies result in Ebay sellers flocking to other sites such as Amazon.com to sell items or it adversely affects Ebay's revenues you can expect to see some of these new policies adjusted or done away with.

How are Feedback scores calculated?

The way that feedback scores are calculated on Ebay is you receive +1 point to your feedback score for each positive comment and rating left for you. 0 points to your feedback score for each neutral comment and rating left for you.-1 point to your feedback score for each negative comment and rating left for you.

You also receive feedback stars that also indicate your feedback status and is based on the number of feedbacks you have received. Feedback stars are located to the right of a member's user ID. You receive different color stars based on the amount of points you have accumulated:

Yellow star = 10 to 49 points, Blue star = 50 to 99 points, Turquoise = 100 to 499 points. Purple star =500 to 999 points, Red star = 1,000 to 4,999 points, Green star = 5,000 to 9,999 points, Yellow shooting star = 10,000 to 24,999 points, Turquoise shooting star = 25,000 to 49,000 points, Purple shooting Star = 50,000 to 99,999 points, Red Shooting Star= 100,000 or higher.

My Ebay Story (Continued)

To continue back to my Ebay story, my feedback rating at this point in my Ebay career was 100%. I was 41 for 41. Forty-one transactions and forty-one positive feedbacks. Paying for auctions really fast helped me in establishing my reputation and street credibility on Ebay. This was important because the goal was to be on the other side of the equation as a seller making money.

Super Tip: You must build your feedback rating. Feedback is a great way to establish you as a trustable, honest and fair person. Ebay requires that you have a feedback rating of 10 to do "buy it now" auctions. However, if you use Paypal as an accepted form of payment for all of your auctions, you only need a feedback rating of 5. In addition you need a feedback rating of 30 to do dutch auctions, which means you can sell more than 2 of any single identical item. You can buy a lot consisting of 50 items at a deep discount and sell them all at once to 50 different buyers.

Super Tip: A quick way to build your feedback rating on Ebay is to buy inexpensive products like for example costume jewelry. Don't spend more than $2 or $3 an item unless of course you like it. Once you've receive your item from the seller immediately contact them through the Ebay email system and ask them can they leave you positive feedback and you will do the same for them. Some people may view this as buying feedback, but I call it marketing 101.

Registering as an Ebay seller

Registering as a seller on Ebay is simple. All you need to have is a checking account and a credit or debit card. Ebay uses this information as a security measure to both confirm your identity and to ensure that you don't forget to pay your seller fees. They actually require you to choose a form of payment. You could either have your seller fees automatically deducted from your checking account, debit card or credit card.

Now that I knew how Ebay was going to receive their payment from me as a seller, I needed to establish the most convenient and easiest way for me to receive payment from winning bidders of the auctions that I planned to list. I chose Paypal.

Paypal

Paypal is an Ebay owned company that allows its registered members to send and receive money online to anyone in the world who has an email address. Registration is free. All you need to have is a checking account to establish a personal account. However, with this personal account you are limited. You are able to send money online without any problem however, you can only receive money if your banking account is confirmed and someone sends you money with funds already in their Paypal account.

A personal account doesn't allow you to receive credit card payments. To be able to accept credit card payments from people who are buying items from you regardless if it's from Ebay or your own website etc, you need to have a Paypal business premier or merchant account. The requirements are either registering your debit or credit card along with your checking account with Paypal. The checking account you registered must be confirmed in order for you to receive credit card payments.

Paypal Confirmation Process

This is how the confirmation process works. When you register your checking account with Paypal they immediately make two small deposits into your bank account. You must then find out from your bank or check your bank statement for the actual amounts deposited. Once you have found these amounts, you must then go to the Paypal website and log into your account.

Once you have logged into your account, look on the left or right side of the web page and you will see a link that says confirm your bank account. Click on this link and you then will be prompted to insert the amounts that were deposited. When you have correctly indicated the two amounts deposited, your Paypal account becomes confirmed.

This confirmation process is a measure of security for Paypal and its members because it establishes that this is in fact your checking account and the address that you gave to Paypal when you registered was valid.

A Clear Understanding of Paypal

It is important to note that Paypal charges the business premier or merchant account a fee to receive money. They charge 2.9% of the amount that was sent to you plus a .30 cent transaction fee. This is automatically deducted from the gross amount sent. This small fee shouldn't matter to you at all. Consider it a small toll that you have to pay to get to your destination of developing an income stream from Ebay.

Also it is important to know the ways to access your money once you have received a Paypal payment. Option #1- you could transfer the balance in your Paypal account to your banking account. This process takes up to three to four business days and it is free.

Option#2 – you could request a check from Paypal for the balance in your account. This process takes 1-2 weeks and it cost $1.50. Option #3 –you could use your Paypal debit card to withdraw money from your account. There is a fee of one dollar to do this. To be eligible to receive a Paypal debit card, you must be a member for at least 30 days and you must provide your social security number.

One of the greatest things about Paypal is that they allow you to link your Paypal account to your Ebay account. This linkage enables you to efficiently manage all of your business activities on Ebay. To link the two accounts, simply register as a member on Ebay and Paypal. Once this is done, log into your Paypal account. After you have logged into your Paypal account, hover the pointer of your mouse on the link that says profile you will see drop down choices. Click on the link that says "more options" you will be led to the profile summary page.

On the profile summary page click on where it says "My Selling Tools". You will see a caption and a link that says "Ebay ID" click on it. You will see an "add" button which allows you to add your Ebay account. Click on this "Add" button and enter in your Ebay user name and click the submit button and your Paypal account is now linked to your Ebay account.

Managing Your Activities on Ebay

The way to manage your activities on Ebay is to first log into your Ebay account and then click on the link on top of the page called "My Ebay. "My Ebay" is a central hub where you can manage all your activities on Ebay including buying, selling, feedback and account preferences.

Under the caption entitled "All Selling" if you click on the link called "active" you can watch all of your items that you have listed in various auctions. Here you can keep track of how many bids you have received and the time remaining on each and every auction you have listed.

Here is an example of how the linkage between your Ebay and Paypal accounts would work for you. Let's say you listed seven different items in seven different auctions and all of the auctions end in three days. When the auctions have ended these are the following results. Five items sold and two did not. You got paid through Paypal for three of the items and the remaining two you are awaiting payment for. You can review all of these results in My Ebay.

When you click on the link entitled " sold" under the all selling heading in My Ebay, you will be able to see what you have sold, which in this case is the five items. You will also be able to view the date of the sale and the final sales price. When your buyer has paid for their item, you will see a dollar sign logo next to the sold item. You will also see under the caption called "actions" a drop down menu with the following choices: printing the shipping label, add tracking number, marked as shipped as well as other options.

The print shipping label option allows you to purchase your postage right on Ebay and the amount the postage or the shipping cost if you're using UPS is automatically deducted from your Paypal account since it is linked to your Ebay account. When you print your shipping label simply click on the print shipping label link and you are taken to a page that's where you would have to select the carrier (usps or ups), enter the weight and the package size and select the shipment options.

The shipment options include selecting the date that you are going to mail the package, and the option of purchasing insurance. Once you have made your choices confirm your purchase and a browser window will open up with your shipping label and all you have to do is print it from your computer. Once this is done your shipping tracking number will become visible in the Ebay menu and your buyer will also be able to simultaneously see it in their Ebay account. How neat is that?

Ebay's Buyer and Seller Protection Program

Ebay has a program to protect sellers as well as buyers. Essentially Ebay's buyer protection program covers items purchased on Ebay with eligible payment methods that are not received or not as described in the listing. Ebay's seller protection program is offered to all

Ebay Sellers for buyer claims filed in the Ebay Resolution Center. To qualify for the Ebay seller protection program a seller must:

- Communicate proactively with your buyer throughout the transaction.
- Ship items within 7 days of the stated handling time on your listing. For pre-ordered or made-to-order goods, ship within the timelines stated in your listing.
- Use a shipping method that provides tracking information and/or valid delivery confirmation to the address in the Paypal transaction details or Ebay order details page.
- Provide signature confirmation for transactions over $250.
- Retain your shipping documentation
- Respond to the Ebay resolution process in a timely manner.

The Seller's Mentality

I don't know about you, but I'd rather be the guy that's selling the tickets to the ballgame, because chances are if the teams that are playing are any good, or provide exceptional entertainment value, the stadium should be filled to capacity. If the stadium is filled to capacity, the person who has sold all those tickets made a lot of money. Don't get me wrong I enjoy going to a good game or two, but I know that the person who owns the team and sold me the ticket is probably rich, where as all I got was to see a good game. Knowing this equation, I began to think of any and everything I could sell on Ebay.

Some of the ideas I came up with were selling some old music equipment and vinyl records that I no longer had any use for. I then gave my mother a call to find out if she had any items that she wanted to discard. She gave me a lot of brand name things she no longer had any use for: Gucci handbags, Gucci shoes, designer clothes etc. One by one I listed these items for sale on Ebay.

On Ebay, there are two ways to list an auction:

Online auction- Most Ebay auctions follow this format. A seller offers an item(s) and sets an opening bid price in an auction with an ending time frame of one day, three days, five days, seven days or ten days. The seller has the option to set a reserve price-which is basically a hidden minimum price that they would accept for the item(s). They also have the choice of setting a "buy it now" price as described earlier. Buyers then visit the seller's auction and bid on the item(s). When the auction is over, the high bidder wins the right to purchase the item(s).

Fixed price auction- a fixed price auction is when a seller in their auction sets a price that is "fixed". This enables the buyer(s) to purchase the item(s) without having to wait or bid as in a regular auction style listing. Also in this format, the seller can choose an auction duration of one day, two days, three days, five days, seven days, ten days,30 days or good till cancelled.

Ebay requires that you have a feedback rating of 10 to do fixed price auctions for a quantity of one. However, if you use Paypal as an accepted form of payment for all of your auctions, you only need a feedback rating of 5.

To create a fixed price listing with a quantity of two or more, you must have a feedback rating of 30 or more and be a registered user for at least 14 days (or be ID verified). What is Id verification? Id verification establishes your proof of identity, so others will trust you as their trading partner. Your personal information is crosschecked against credit business databases for consistency.

Please note that Id verification is not a credit check. When your information has been successfully verified you will receive a logo indicating that you have been Id verified. This process cost $5 and is charged to your Ebay account.

Title, Description, Shipping And Price

The keys to getting many potential bidders to visit your auction on Ebay are the keywords that you use in your title and description for the item. For example, the title that I used for the Gucci handbag that my mother gave to me read: Authentic Vintage Gucci Handbag. The keywords in this title are Gucci, Handbag, Authentic and Vintage. So anytime an auction surfer typed in a combination of those keywords in their search for an item, my auction came up.

I would suggest to you that before you list an item on Ebay, search the keywords you plan to use in the title to see how many listings come up. If the results are few or none at all, you should try using different keywords in your title unless you have a very unique item for sale. Also I would check for any misspellings.

On the other hand if there are many listings, chances are you chose some good keywords. Also I might add, I happen to get lucky that my keyword was Gucci and that is a highly popular brand name on Ebay. In fact, I noticed that most of the Gucci items had bids on them. So I was destined to be successful with my Gucci auctions.

I would strongly recommend before you decide to sell a product on Ebay that you search to see if that product is commercially viable. For example, is the product that you intend to sell receiving a lot of bids in other auctions? Also check the price that the product is selling for and read the description to get a few good ideas for your listing. Last but not least, study the various seller's offers and strategies. This will enable you to get to know your competition.

After I settled on a title for my Gucci auction, I began with my description, which was brief, accurate and honest. It read:

You are bidding on a very unique used mint condition vintage Gucci Handbag made in the early 70's. This bag would look great with any wardrobe. It has a red and blue canvas strip down the middle with the trademark GG monogram imprinted all over the bag. It also has a zipper compartment on the front of the bag, with a gold GG logo emblem also attached to the zipper for extra class. The bag's measurements are height=7", length is 10", dimension=3" and the strap is 19" long. I guarantee that this bag is 100% authentic. Shipping is $10.75 U.S.A., $12 Canada and $25 for Great Britain and anywhere else. I accept Paypal only. Payment is due within 48 hours of auction ending.

Although Paypal is highly convenient and to me is the best possible choice to receive your payment from your buyers, you can choose other payment options such as a credit card and other Ebay approved payment vendors like Propay, Skrill and Paymate. This can be done when you are adding the details to your auction.

Ebay allows you to upload a picture(s) of the item to your auction. The first picture is free and any additional picture incurs a charge. If you have your own web hosting, you can host your own pictures avoiding any fees. Having pictures in your auction is a must, because as the saying goes "a picture is worth a thousand words". It allows the bidders to connect with the item that you are selling aesthetically. A basic digital camera is sufficient to take great pictures of your items that you intend to list on Ebay.

Here are some quick tips on how to take great pictures for Ebay

- Make sure that you use the proper lighting when taking pictures of your item.

- Try to use a background that will contrast well.

- Take pictures at different angles to give bidders a complete view and in depth representation of the item.

- Avoid background clutter.

Quick tutorial on how to upload your pictures to your Ebay auctions:

- Take a picture of your item with your digital camera.

- Save the picture on your computer. (remember where you saved it at)

- When you get to the create your listing page click on the add picture button and another browser window will open.

- Click the browse button to select the picture you want to upload from your computer.

- A dialogue box displays, enabling you to navigate to the folder that contains the picture on your computer.

- Click the picture file that you want.

- Click the open or ok button. This selects the picture file to be uploaded when you click the upload all button.

- Click the upload button and you are finished.

Back to my Gucci auction, I set the starting bidding price of the Gucci bag at $1.00. I did this to encourage a lot of bids on the item. I knew that the bidding price would be driven up automatically, because the initial bid price was low. It didn't cost bidders much to "enter in the bidding game".

After uploading my picture of the Gucci bag, I hit the submit listing button and my seven day auction began. To my surprise after submitting my auction I received 5 bids on the bag within five hours. By day number six the amount of bids I received was up to 29.

This was amazing to watch, I was just salivating over the profits that I would be making, so I continued to watch the last 5 minutes of the auction. Two bidders in particular were bidding back and forth, so I was sure in my mind that either one of them would be the winning bidder. It seemed to me that the other bidders had dropped out of the bidding race completely. Low and behold the auction came to a close.

The two bidders that were engaged in a bidding war both had lost! To my amazement an unknown bidder came out of nowhere and beat out the other two bidders in the last remaining seconds. I was elated, the final auction price was $357. The cost associated with this auction was the following. Ebay charged me a listing fee of .30 cents and a final valuation fee of $10.44, bringing my total Ebay fees for this auction to $10.77.

Final valuation fee

The final valuation fee is based on the final sale price of the item. It was calculated in this particular auction the following way. 5.25% was charged to the first $25 of the final price. This amounted to $1.31. For the remaining $332 ($357-$25) 2.75 % was applied. This amounted to $9.13 ($332 x %2.75). The final valuation fee totaled $10.44 ($1.31+$9.13).

The winning bidder immediately sent me a Paypal payment of $367.75 ($357 + $10.75 shipping). Paypal immediately deducted their service fee of $10.96 ($367.75 X 2.9% service fee plus a 30 cents transaction fee). My total fees including both Paypal and Ebay totaled $21.73. My profit was an astounding $335.27 from one single auction.

I want you to stop and think for a second and take out your calculator and multiply that $335.27 profit that I made by 30. Your calculator should say $10,058.10. Is it possible to sell 30 items with a profit of 335.27 per item on Ebay to make a quick 10G's? Of course it is!!!

To accomplish this, all you have to do is utilize the powerful wholesale information I supplied you with in this book and find the right combination of products that will produce this result. This involves some testing to see what works. Once you have figured out what works, implement a system to list auctions that will lead you to achieving your financial goals. Remember, when setting these goals, it is important to always

THINK BIG.

Unfortunately for me my mother didn't have 30 more Gucci bags. However, from the one that I did sell, I used the proceeds to take her to dinner. She absolutely loved it as any mom would.

Super Tip: The journey of 1,000 miles begins with the first step. Look around your house or apartment for things that have value that you are no longer using and take your first step as a seller on Ebay by listing and selling these items.

The Seller's Experiment

I continued to put items up for sale on Ebay. Some of these items I listed as fixed price auctions, others I listed as regular online auctions where people were allowed to compete and bid. I had success both ways. In instances where I did not have success with the items that I listed, (I received no bids at all) I wanted to know the reason so I did some research.

For example, I had listed a popular pair of Diesel jeans with an opening bid of $79.99 and a "buy it now" price of $99.99 at the time when Diesel jeans were hot on Ebay. This auction received no bids at all, so I began to check the competition's auctions to see if they were experiencing the same results.

This is what I discovered. 95% of the Diesel jeans had bids on them!!! So I checked to see if there were any major differences between my auction and theirs. The title, description and pictures were similar. However, the major difference was the opening bid price. They started their opening auctions at .01 to $1.00 where as my auctions began at $79.99.

As I mentioned previously, to become a great seller you have to know the psychology of buying and the buyer. The other sellers instantly got bids on their Diesel jeans, because they started their opening bids low and bidders weren't afraid to bid on these low amounts. Come on would you be afraid to place a bid of a penny on an item that retails for $150? Of course not! You're only risking a penny and technically if no one else bid on this item, you win.

When buying people have limits as to what they would pay for an item. Conversely, these limits vary with each individual. One person's limit may be a penny, another person's limit may $50 and another $100. As each person enters their different bid amounts, this has the effect of driving the initial bid price up and attracting other bidders. It is human nature for people to conform, so when potential bidders see several bids on an item already, they feel comfortable enough to bid. So they bid, driving the price up even further.

Needless to say I relisted the Diesel jeans again, but this time I set the opening bid price at $1.00. To ensure that these jeans sold at a profitable price, I set a reserve price of $79.99. Bidders did not see this price because it was hidden from them. The reserve price is the lowest price you are willing to sell an item for. Ebay charges a fee for this, but you are refunded if the item has successfully sold.

The Diesel jeans sold the second time around because of the valuable lessons I learned and applied. I experimented more and more as a seller with favorable results, but now I wanted to go for the kill. I wanted to make more money, so I devised a strategy. I used the Ebay search engine to find out the hottest selling items. I started off searching the top designer brands for clothing and accessories. Here are some of those brand names that I searched:

Tommy Hilfiger, Betsey Johnson, Polo by Ralph Lauren, Ambercrombie and Fitch, The Limited, Express,Victoria's Secret, Guess, Nautica, Fubu, Rocawear, Phat Farm, Mecca, Triple Five Soul, Sean John, Akademiks, Enyce.

In addition, I also did a search on the various types of electronic products including computers. I searched computer and computers accessories, dvd players, karaoke machines, home theatre systems, car accessories.

The list goes on, I just wanted to give you an idea on how extensive my research was. I spent the time and effort because I knew it would result in me making a lot of money. Research can translate to a lot of dollars for you also. All of the items that I just mentioned to you for both clothing & accessories and electronics had plenty bids on them.

It dawned on me that if I obtained the information on how to acquire these products at wholesale or even below wholesale prices, purchased them and resold them on Ebay, the money would pour in. Better yet, I posed this question to myself, what if I didn't have to spend the money upfront to acquire these items?

Super Tip: A quick, easy and detailed way to search for possible items to sell on Ebay is by using Terapeak. Terapeak is a service that helps sellers perform research on products, trends, categories and auctions across Ebay. The service helps you find what kind of products are being sold on Ebay to help you figure out if you're entering a profitable market. Terapeak also helps you get new ideas on what to promote and how to promote it.

Dropshipment

Dropshipping was the "no money down" secret I used to become a powerseller on Ebay. I found the ultimate answer and solution to that question I mentioned previously of "what if I didn't have to spend the money upfront to acquire these items?" Dropshipping requires no stocking of inventory and no upfront costs.

This is how it works:
You simply copy the images and descriptions of the product you want to sell from the dropshipment wholesaler's website. After that you mark up the price of the product to what you think the market will allow. Then you would list that product on Ebay.

You don't have to buy the product. You only purchase the product when the customer has paid you for it. When that product has sold, the customer pays you through Paypal. When the customer has paid you, you then forward the customer's name and address along with a payment through Paypal to the dropshipment wholesaler for the product that the customer ordered. The money left over is your profit!!!

The dropshipment wholesaler ships the product to your customer in your name. Now how easy is that? You don't have to stock any inventory, ship any products and you don't need money to make money. You simply list the product on Ebay, go to sleep and let the bidders go into a frenzy!

If you want access to a company that has a database consisting of scam free wholesalers and dropshipment companies visit the following link below:

http://www.worldwidebrands.com/r/?r=1&kbid=16861

I used three dropshippers in particular to become an Ebay powerseller. The first one was Premier Closeout and their website address is www.hotbuy4u.com.

From this particular dropshipper, I was able to sell dvd players, karaoke machines, portable dvd players, digital cameras, toys, computer accessories, home theatre systems, car accessories and much much more. I suggest that you check out their website.

The second dropshipper that I used was Maxam Wholesale at www.maxamwholesale.com. They have a free catalog, you can call them at (800) 350-4495. You can also view the products that they have by visiting their website.

The third dropshipper I used was the Specialty Merchandise Corporation. Their website address is www.smcorp.com. They have thousands of gifts, toys, novelties and collectibles which are big on Ebay. In order to purchase merchandise from Specialty Merchandise Corporation, you have to become a member. The membership fee is $300. However, this fee is refunded after you have purchased $5,000 in merchandise from them.

My first dropshipment sale on Ebay was a Polaroid digital camera. I bought it for $29.99 from www.hotbuy4u.com. I listed it on Ebay as a fixed price auction for $89.99 and passed the $6.25 shipping charge to the customer. After Ebay fees of $3.10 and Paypal fees of $2.91, I made a profit of $53.99.

I made money without having to use my own money and I didn't have to stock any inventory or go to the post office. I created money out of thin air by just clicking my mouse a few times. In a week's time I sold 8 digital cameras like the one I just mentioned, 6 Karaoke machines, 3 portable DVD players for a net profit of $916.

During the same week I was also selling clothing. I bought at below wholesale prices 12 pairs of men's Diesel jeans and 12 pairs of women's Seven jeans. The style of the men's Diesel jeans that I listed were very popular, they were called Zathan. They were a low rise boot cut jean. The style of the women's seven jeans were also very popular, they were the "A pocket" style, low rise and boot cut.

The percentages were in my favor that these jeans were going to sell within a week. My confidence was based on the tracking of 15 different auctions that offered for sale men's Diesel Zathan jeans and women's Seven jeans. These auctions all ended successfully, 15 auctions resulted in 15 sales. The conversion ratio was 100%.

Armed with these facts, I listed these jeans for sale on Ebay and I achieved the same winning results. This is a very important lesson for you. The lesson is: before you get your heart dead set on selling a particular item on Ebay check out and analyze other auctions that are selling the same item. This will enable you to gauge the market place to determine your pricing and positioning.

The wholesale price that I paid for both the Diesel and Seven jeans were $45 per pair for a total of $1,080 (24 pairs of jeans multiplied by $45). My gross profit from the sale of these jeans was $2,700. My net profit was $2,510 after Ebay and Paypal fees. I repeated these same successful steps with dropshipping and selling clothing for the next 4 weeks with outstanding results. In 30 days I made $11,789!

Do I think you can make $11,789 like I did in 30 days? That's entirely up to you. It all depends upon your desire and your willingness to do the proper research and due diligence in regards to finding the right profitable product to sell on Ebay.

I'm detailing my Ebay auction experiences so that you will be able to leapfrog your way over the competition in a short period of time. It is my firm belief that you do not have to "stand in line" in order to achieve success. It's all about making quantum leaps. That should be your mindset. This mindset and my success on Ebay allowed me to leave my 9 to 5 job in a rapid fashion.

Conversely, Ebay is all about trends and trends change over time. The previous examples that I provided to you like for instance my Diesel jeans auctions represented seizing on a particular hot trend at the right time for maximum profit. That should be your theme and mantra:

"Seizing on hot trends at the right time for maximum profits"

Here is another tool that will help you in determining "What's hot on Ebay". This tool is called Ebay Pulse which gives you a snapshot of daily trends and popular searches. You can access it here: http://pulse.Ebay.com/

Super Tip: Ebay's turbo lister is a free listing tool that allows you to list multiple items and upload to Ebay in bulk.

Making money on Ebay while you sleep!

Quick side bar: The one thing that gets my adrenaline flowing on Ebay is having and selling a hot product where the demand is so strong that there is an absolute frenzy for it. When this occurs, I buy as much of this product as I possibly can, because I want to feed this frenzy as well as stuff my pockets.

Timing is key. So without hesitation, I quickly list several of these hot items in different fixed price auctions just right before I go to bed at night. I use the fixed price auction format, because there is no waiting or bidding involved for the buyer or I. I love this equation of quick purchases equals quick cash.

In the wee hours of the night while I am asleep in my pajamas (sometimes I wear those things), I am making money. The ultimate high for me is when I wake up and log into my Paypal account to view the killing that I made while I was asleep. So my advice to you is once you get that "hot product" seize the moment and "run with it". Run straight to the bank!

Open your Ebay store

There are several advantages in opening up a store on Ebay:

- You are able to cross-promote your merchandise.
- There are lower listing fees and longer listing periods.

- You are able to customize and personalize your store.
- When you open an Ebay store you have a unique url that will be picked up by the search engines. You can promote your url online or offline.
- Your Ebay store is open for business 24 hours a day, 7 days a week and 365 days out of the year. This will enable you to do other important things like shopping, sleeping or having sex.
- Customize and personalize your store- Ebay allows the store seller to create custom headers and store front pages using html.
- One of the super benefits of becoming an Ebay store owner is that your store is automatically included in the Ebay store directory, which is promoted to millions of Ebay members.

There are three different Ebay Store levels:

Basic- This level is for sellers who are just starting out. Currently there is a monthly charge of $15.95 per month.

Premium- Designed for medium size sellers who want to grow their online business. The subscription fee for the featured store is currently $49.95 per month.

Anchor- An advance store with solutions for high-volume sellers who want maximum Ebay exposure. The subscription fee for the anchor store is currently $299.95 per month.

To open an Ebay store simply go to Ebay's home page and click on the link Ebay stores. Then click on the link

"Open a Store" and follow the necessary steps to set up your store.

What if the winning bidder doesn't pay me?

Everything I discussed about Ebay up to this point was based on the assumption that you would get paid by the winning bidder when you've successfully sold an item in an auction. However, let me caution you. There are times when the winning bidder does not pay. When this occurs, the following are the steps you must take in order to receive a final valuation fee credit from Ebay.

The seller must file an unpaid item dispute with Ebay. The seller must then wait 4 days after the auction ending to file an unpaid item dispute. Ebay allows up to 32 days after the transaction date to report an unpaid item. If you try to file an unpaid item dispute after the 32 days forget about it, your toast.

Once you have filed the unpaid dispute Ebay alerts the non-paying bidder. The non-paying bidder then is afforded the opportunity to open a dialogue with you and discuss the matter through Ebay's dispute console.

At this point, the buyer will either pay or not pay to resolve the issue. The buyer has 4 days to respond to this dispute. If they choose not to pay or you feel that the buyer is stonewalling you, you have a right to end all dialogue and close the dispute and indicate to Ebay that you still haven't received payment and they will instantly give you credit for the final valuation fee that they charged you for the sale.

To recall, the final valuation fee is the fee that Ebay charges you when you've sold an item. However, I must note that Ebay does not refund the listing fee. I have a listing fee and final valuation fee story that I must mention. It has something to do with what I call seller envy. Success sometimes breeds envy. Envy can lead to sabotage. I received an email asking me why was I selling digital cameras cheaper than what other Ebay sellers were selling them for?

The email went on to say that other sellers couldn't compete with the low prices that I was offering, so it was suggested that I raise my prices. Now of course I wasn't going to do that, so I ignored the email completely. The next thing you know all my auctions that were listed as "buy it now" were ended by the same bidder.

The total final valuation fees charged to my account as a result of this sabotage was about $400. In addition, there were listing fees charges totaling $275. Ebay charged my credit card $675. I was charged in full because the billing cycle ended the following day after the sabotage. So there wasn't enough time to go through the non-paying bidder dispute process. Of course I was livid, how could Ebay charge me these fees and my auctions were blatantly sabotaged? I contacted Ebay by email because at the time you could not contact them by telephone.

I told them that someone registered as a member on Ebay with the intentions of sabotaging my auctions. This was not paranoia. At that particular time it was so easy to register as a buyer on Ebay, all you needed was an email address. You didn't need a checking account or a credit card like you do when registering as a seller. There wasn't any stringent verification, so essentially you could make up a fictitious name, telephone number and address and buy on Ebay.

Ebay's response was that listing fees were non refundable (so basically, I was out of $275) and that I had to file a non paying dispute and go through that process to recoup the final valuation fees. Then Ebay instructed me to refer to the user agreement that I agreed to upon becoming a member. To be honest with you, I only read the first two sentences of the user agreement. I mean who reads these things and remembers them anyway?

Lesson: Read the entire user agreement for Ebay and Paypal as well as any other entity. User agreements spell out your rights as a member and explains what you are liable for in the event that something goes wrong.

To tell you the truth, I wanted to just dispute the charges with my credit card company via chargeback, but Ebay's policy views this as "an attempt to circumvent paying for fees". If I would have taken this route Ebay would have suspended my account. I tell you this story not to scare you but to remind you that Ebay although it is an absolute goldmine, is not exempt from Murphy's Law. I would recommend that if you encounter something similar, just suck it up, move on and continue to make money.

How to deal with negative feedback

I suggest that you be accurate and honest in describing an item in your listing. Provide as many details as possible. If an item has a scratch or a slight tear, make sure that you've mentioned it. Also, you should indicate whether or not an item that you are selling is refundable .Ebay now makes it mandatory that you do so.

After the winning bidder has paid you, make sure you ship the item in a timely fashion. Following these procedures gives you a peace of mind, while providing satisfaction to your customer. However, you can't control the opinions of customers.

For the most part if transactions go smoothly, customers will leave you positive feedback, but sometimes on rare occasion you may encounter the opposite even though you followed the procedures.

Yes, I'm talking about the dreaded negative feedback that someone leaves for you, which in most cases is a permanent mark on your feedback profile. Every time you list an item for sale potential bidders if they check your feedback profile will see this negative comment even though it may be undeserving.

Ebay rarely removes negative feedback. The only instances where they will remove negative feedback is if you could prove that the negative feedback is a result of a campaign to harass you, the comments contained extremely vulgar language, a valid court order finding that the disputed feedback is slanderous, libelous, defamatory or otherwise illegal.

The only other hope that you have to remove negative feedback is through your buyer. There are some situations when buyers can revise the feedback comment or rating, or the detailed seller ratings (DSRs) that they've left for a seller. For example, if you the seller fixed the problem with the transaction, or if the buyer accidentally left the wrong feedback. In these situations, sellers can request a feedback revision but the buyer must agree to it.

In the event that you are unsuccessful in having negative feedback removed, understand that this is not the end of the world. Never let someone's negative comments paralyzed you. If 99 people out of 100 left you positive feedback and only 1 person left you negative feedback your feedback rating is still very high at 99%. Ebayers will still continue to do business with you. So life goes on.

Here is one of my great feedback stories. I had listed an Ann Taylor blouse on Ebay and in the description I stated that the color of the blouse was black. When the winning bidder received the item, she contacted me by email and said "obviously you shipped me the wrong colored blouse, the one that you sent me is black and I won the auction for a blue one!"

Of course, I emailed her back and politely told her to go back and reread the description of the auction, it clearly stated that this was an auction for a black blouse from Ann Taylor. She never responded back, so I assumed that she realized that she was mistaken. Wrong assumption! I checked my feedback profile and saw that she left negative feedback. It read "seller sent black blouse, I won an auction for a blue one".

I responded back by leaving her negative feedback which you could do at that time. My comment read "the color of the item was black as described in auction, buyer didn't read description". I had to let the Ebay community know that the buyer wasn't playing with a full deck. Thank God, Ebay places a link to the auction next to the feedback comment left by members. This link leads back to the original auction. Members could clearly see with their own eyes a picture of the black blouse and also read the description where I stated that the color of the blouse was black.

Some other important things you need to know about Ebay

1) On Ebay you can have more than one account. I suggest that you have more than one account. I actually have 3.One I use strictly for buying, the other I use strictly for selling, and the third account I have as a just in case account. Just in case something goes wrong with

the other two accounts. As the saying goes "you don't want to put all your eggs in one basket". To register for additional accounts, all you have to do is register using a different email address. However, all contact information must remain the same.

2) Shill Bidding - Shill bidding involves sellers who bid on their own auction or have someone that they know bidding on their auction without any intention on winning. Shill bidding is done to increase the final price for auctions or to make an auction appear more popular than it really is. This is totally against Ebay rules. Engaging in this type of behavior may result in these actions: Account Suspension, Listing Cancellation, Referral to Law Enforcement.

3) Free relist policy – If your auction ends without a winning buyer or results in an unpaid item, you are eligible under certain circumstances to receive a listing credit when you have relisted that same item and it sells the second time around. To be eligible the following conditions must be met: You must relist the item within 90 days. The starting price for the relisted item must not be greater than the price of the original listing. Both the original listing and the relisting must be in online Auction or fixed Price format. The relisted item must sell the second time if it doesn't you are no longer eligible for a free relist for that particular auction. The relisted item must not have a reserve price if the original auction didn't. If you decide to include a reserve price in the relisted item it can't be greater than the price of the original auction. Only single quantity auctions are eligible.

4) Proxy bidding- This is how the Ebay bidding system works. When you enter a bid on Ebay you are informing Ebay of the maximum amount that you intend to pay for an item. Ebay then bids incrementally on your behalf by comparing your bid to other bids place on the item, using only as much of your bid as is necessary to maintain your high bid position. If another bid is higher than your maximum amount you were effectively outbid. However, if no other bidder has a higher maximum, you win the item. Possibly paying significantly less than your maximum bid.

5) Vero – Vero stands for verified rights owners. They are intellectual property owners who are given the right by Ebay to report an item that infringes upon their intellectual rights. If a vero member decides someone has violated their rights, they can unilaterally cancel the auctions of other sellers. For example, if you list a product from Nike and if Nike decides that this isn't an authentic product, they have the right to cancel your auction. If you list these type of infringing items repeatedly, your account will be suspended.

6) Ebay seller fees- Ebay seller fees are due according to your billing cycle date which is either going to be on the 15th or the last day of the month. The billing cycle date is determined at the time you have created your Ebay seller's account.

7) As of late October 2008, Ebay no longer allows sellers to accept checks and money orders as a form of payment. Sellers can only offer buyers an approved online payment service such as Paypal, Propay or other approved Ebay vendors. In addition to these changes Ebay of course has made changes to its fee structure regarding insertion fees

and final valuation fees. They are calculated different than what I mentioned here in describing my earlier Ebay experiences.

Trader Assistant

If you don't want to personally sell your Ebay items or you prefer to sell items for other Ebayers you can use or become a trader assistant. Trading assistants are experienced Ebay sellers who will sell your items on Ebay for a fee.

The main benefit of using a trader assistant in helping you sell your items on Ebay is that they do all of the work. They handle every aspect of the selling process from listing an item to shipping it to the buyer. How wonderful of a concept is that? You just hand off your item to the trading assistant and go play golf, ride a bicycle or whatever it is that you do and the trading assistant will collect payment from the buyer, deduct any fees you owe, and pass the rest on to you.

To become an Ebay Trading Assistant, be listed in the Trading Assistant Directory, and gain access to marketing materials, you must agree to and abide by the Ebay Trading Assistant User Agreement and you must reside in the U.S.

In addition, you must:

- Have an Ebay account in good standing at all times.

- Have sold at least ten (10) items on Ebay in the previous three (3) months and maintain 10 sales per 3-month period.

- Maintain a minimum feedback score of 100, with at least 98% positive, at all times.

- Abide by the terms of the Trading Assistant Style Guide.

To find a trader assistant located near you, all you would have to do is look in the trader assistant's directory located on Ebay's website. The trader assistant's directory is easy to find, just click on the help link on the website and type in the search box"trader assistant". You will then enter your street address, city, state and zip code. After that you have to choose from the drop down menu the category that your item fits under.

In searching for a trader's assistant you have the option to choose whether you want to view the trader assistants who offer a staffed drop-off location or a pick up service. After you have made your choice, click on the search button. The results page will list all of the trading assistants in your area. It will even break down the distance they are from your location.

If you can enjoy making money selling things for other people, why not become a trader's assistant yourself?

Super Tip: Check the various stores in your area and see if they offering great deals on products that you know would sell well on Ebay. Make a deal with them to sell their products. Take a picture of the items, price them at a profit, then sell them on Ebay. This doesn't require up front money because you will only buy the product from them when you have collected the money from your customer.

Repeat Business

The main foundation of any business and its most valuable asset is the customers that it has. Without the customer, you essentially have no business. When you have obtained a customer from Ebay it is in your best interest to continue to cultivate a relationship with that customer through continuous contact which enables you to make more offers. Making more enticing offers and discounts to the customer will result in more sales. Making more sales will fatten your pockets.

Although Ebay rules dictate that you can't make offers to Ebay members through the Ebay medium, they have no jurisdiction that precludes you from making offers outside of Ebay once you have obtained the customer. Imagine they had such a rule that restricted you from making offers after you have obtained the customer? It would be monopolistic and against so-called free trade.

There are two ways you could stay in contact with your Ebay customers. One way is by direct mail, the other way is through permission based email marketing. For example, when you ship your package you could include a letter thanking the customer for the purchase and in this letter you can also indicate that you have other neat nifty products for sale on your website.

At your website, you should have a FREE signup for discount products. In order for the customer to receive your discount offers, they would have to include their email address allowing you to market to them by the way of an autoresponder.

Autoresponders send out emails at different intervals automatically. There are numerous autoresponder companies on the internet however I suggest you choose one that has a double opt-in feature. The double opt-in is basically the customer has to confirm that they are giving you permission to market to them by email. There are spamming laws in effect and this protects you from their tentacles. Aweber is the autoresponder company that I use and they are the top provider in the industry. You can visit them at the following link:

http://www.aweber.com/

Creating your own website involves a series of steps:

The first step is choosing your domain name. For example, makeprofitsnow.com.

The second step is choosing a hosting provider. A hosting company allows you for a monthly fee to maintain your website on their server. Godaddy.com and Web.com are two great hosting providers that you can use.

After registering your domain and choosing your hosting company, it is now time for the designing of your website. Your website doesn't have to be fancy or complex, just simple and easy to navigate. If you have web master skills, needless to say you would design your own website. However, if you don't have these skills there are several ways to accomplish this task.

If you want to design your website yourself without having to master html programming there are several website designing software that allows you to do just that. I will recommend one it's called Dreamweaver.

If you want a webmaster to design your website, I suggest that you go to www.ifreelance.com and offer your website creation project up for competitive bidding. Ifreelance is a great service that allows you to connect with freelance professionals from around the world.

Once you have created your website and it is up and running you can direct your Ebay customers as well as other potential customers outside of Ebay to your website. Your Ebay customers have already bought from you and if they were satisfied with your product and service, they will more than likely buy from you again. This is the science of repeat business. In addition, they will also provide great word of mouth and your business will grow exponentially.

Driving your Ebay customers to your website shouldn't be the only way you obtain customers for your website business. It is imperative that you employ other effective methods. One method is using pay per click advertising most notably Google Adwords.

Super Tip: Never ever under any circumstances include in your Ebay auctions a link that will lead to your website. This is a violation of Ebay rules and will result in cancellation of your listing. In addition, it is also against Ebay rules to mention your website address in your auction.

The Secrets of Making $10,000 on Ebay in 30 days

Can you really consistently make $10,000 a month or more on Ebay? Of course you can! You just need a $10,000 a month or more Ebay money making blue print from an Ebay powerseller like myself who is actually doing it on a consistent basis.

You need to know the right cutting edge information as well as the secrets that will enable you to accomplish this rather easy goal from my point of view. Having said that here are those jealously guarded secrets and that Ebay money making blue print revealed.

Strategy

In the masterful book Art of War, Chinese military general Sun Tzu reveals that "every battle is won before it is ever fought". So how do you win a battle before it's ever fought? The answer is with strategy. You see if you meticulously plan and have a concrete strategy before you embark on your journey to becoming an Ebay powerseller who consistently makes $10,000 a month or more you will win that battle if you effectively execute.

Trust me, it is indeed a battle going against other Ebay sellers with the same money making goals as yours. Sellers who will in fact will be selling the same exact products as you in most cases. They will even sell their products at a lower price just to make a sale or they may get that product at a cheaper wholesale price allowing them to sell it at a lower price than you.

When this happens and it will because there is competition in the marketplace rather than tuck your tail in, wimp out and run for the hills I will show you a strategy that will enable you to outsmart your competition. How valuable would that information be to you? To be able to crush the competition and in the process make a boat load of cash?

If you are prepared in mind, body, and soul to make your quantum leap to Ebay riches quickly without going through the "school of hardknocks" you have to know the fundamentals so let's go over them.

The first thing on your agenda should be to get a business license in your city, state or locality. The reason why it is imperative for you to do so is because most legitimate wholesale and dropshipment companies require you to have a business certificate and tax id number to do business with them. There is really no way around this. You will also need a business license and a tax id # to open a bank account.

Although I can't advise you as to what type of entity you should structure your company as (you should consult with an attorney) I can give you a brief overview of the different types of entities.

Sole Proprietorship- a sole proprietorship is basically a one person company and is simply "you doing business". There isn't any filing requirement to start your business using this structure unless you are using a fictitious or trade name. If you are using a fictitious or trade name you must file a "d/b/a" or doing business as with your state, city or locality. The only types of fees associated with being a sole proprietor are the licensing fees that your city or state or locality charges for doing business.

Tax Consequences of a Sole Proprietorship

The income made by a sole proprietorship is income earned by its owner. In addition, as a sole proprietor, you report your income, expenses, profits and losses on schedule "C" on your federal income tax return. This income is subject to a self-employment tax.

Disadvantages of Sole Proprietorship

One of the disadvantages of a sole proprietorship is there is unlimited liability. If you got sued everything you have personally is at risk. There is really nothing shielding your personal assets. If your business goes bankrupt, you must file for personal bankruptcy protection to avoid the business debts.

General Partnership

A general partnership is an entity that is formed with two or more parties. No paperwork needs to be filed to create a partnership. In fact, it can be formed with a simple handshake. However, it is better to have a partnership agreement that spells out the terms of the partnership. If there is no partnership agreement then the partnership is governed by state law. The majority of the states in the U.S. have adopted the Uniform Partnership act which consists of a set of rules of how partnerships should act if they don't have a formal agreement.

Liability of a General Partnership

A general partnership has no liability protection for partners. Partners are jointly liable for any acts of negligence. So whether or not a person in a partnership committed a negligent act (someone else may have done it) he or she is still personally liable for that act.

Tax Consequences of a General Partnership

The general partnership itself doesn't pay taxes it simply files an I.R.S. 1065 form. This is only an informational form that summarizes income, expenses and profits and losses of the general partnership business.

A general partnership is treated as a "flow through entity" which means that the profits and losses of the partnership "flows through" to the partners who report their share of income or losses on schedule "E" of their personal income tax returns. The way that this works is that the partnership would send each partner an I.R.S. K-1 form that states their share of the partnership profits or losses.

Limited Partnership

In order to form a limited partnership, the partnership must file a "Certificate of Limited Partnership" with the state in which it is organized. There are two types of partners in a limited partnership. There are the general partner and a limited partner. The general partner controls the day to day operation of the partnership and is liable for all business debt where as a limited partner is not responsible for business debts and/or claims.

Liability of a Limited Partnership

The general partner in a limited partnership have unlimited liability and if a judgment is rendered against the limited partnership and that partnership doesn't have enough assets to cover the claims, the creditor can go after the general partner's personal assets. Sounds risky doesn't it? Well it is!

Now unlike the general partner a limited partner has no liability beyond what they initially invested in the partnership. Creditors can't go after limited partners for the debts of that limited partnership. In addition, limited partners unlike the general partner are not personally liable for acts committed by the general partner unless they participate in management decisions.

Tax Consequences of a Limited Partnership

A limited partnership is also treated as a "flow through entity" for tax purposes. I must point out to you that in "flow through" entities, the owners pay individual income taxes on all net profits of the business. This is the case whether they receive those net profits or not.

Corporation

A corporation is a business entity that carries its own legal status, separate and distinct from its owners. Its' primary advantage is to provide owners with limited liability against business claims. A corporation requires a filing of an articles or "certificate" of incorporation with the state. There are two types of corporations "C" corporations and "S" corporations. An "S" corporation status must be elected.

Tax Consequences of a Corporation

A "C" corporation files an IRS form 1120 and pays taxes on its net income. The primary disadvantage of a "C" corporation is double taxation. Profits are taxed first at corporate tax rates and then again at the individual level when owners receive profits from the corporation in the form of dividends.

An "S" corporation is taxed just like a partnership. It files an information IRS form 1120-S and the profits and losses "flow through" to the shareholders. The S corporation sends each shareholder an IRS K-1 which states the shareholder's share of profits or losses.

Liability of a Corporation

A corporation provides liability protection for its owners (the shareholders). If the corporation was sued, the owners are not personally liable.

Limited Liability Companies

A limited liability company (or "LLC)" is a hybrid cross between a corporation and a partnership. To form a LLC the requirement is that you must file an "articles of organization" with the state. An LLC is owned by its' members or partners and it is governed by its operating agreement.

Liability of a Limited Liability Company

A limited liability company provides protection for its members. The members are not liable beyond their contributions to the company. If the LLC is not able to meet its' debts, the members are not liable for these obligations. In addition, if the LLC is sued the members are not personally liable. An LLC can be "member managed" or "manager-managed".

Tax Consequences of LLC

An LLC is also a "flow through" entity and for single member LLC's the tax reporting requirements are basic. All you have to do is attach an IRS form Schedule C which is a Profit or Loss from a Business to your Form 1040 individual return.

You will also have to file IRS form Schedule SE which is a self-employment tax form. On this schedule you will calculate the amount of self-employment tax owed. This self- employment tax is a combination of Social Security and a Medicare tax.

If there are two or more members of an LLC, then that LLC generally must file its' taxes as a partnership. Like I mentioned previously that requires the LLC to file a form 1065. Income, losses, deductions and credits allocated to each owner for the year are reported on Schedule K of form 1065.

A detailed Schedule K is given to the respective members of the LLC detailing their specific shares of profits and losses. They would then use this information and attach the K-1 to form 1040 of their personal tax return and use it to calculate their personal income tax owed.

Limited Liability Partnerships

LLP's are a special type of partnership designed to provide individual partners with protection against malpractice by other partners in the business. In some states this is known as a registered LLP, or RLLP. LLP's are primarily designed for professions such as doctors, lawyers and accountants.

So there you have it, an overview of the different types of business entities in which to choose from. In running your Ebay business it is imperative that you choose the entity that works best for you. Furthermore, you should also seek the advice of a competent attorney and an accountant before choosing a specific entity.

As a rule of thumb you want the best assessment of the business structure that will allow you to keep a significant amount of your Ebay income while minimizing the taxes that you have to pay to Uncle Sam. It makes no sense to make the money on Ebay and to give a great deal to the IRS just because you didn't choose the appropriate business structure.

Once you have your business name and structure if you haven't joined Ebay yet as a seller do so. Also signup with Paypal and choose the option to open a business account. This will enable you to accept credit cards as well as bank payments for winning bidders of your auction.

Once you have registered with both Ebay and Paypal I want you to join Terapeak. It is imperative that you join Terapeak before you begin selling items or even buying items.

Terapeak enables you to gather the necessary critical intelligence on buying and selling trends on Ebay. Why is this so important? Because as a seller you must know what the Ebay marketplace is willing to pay for an item that you intend to sell. This will enable you to price it accordingly.

In addition, just like the stock market you want to be able to know when to get in and get out when you see that a product has lost its' luster in the marketplace. Furthermore, you will be able to analyze what your competition is doing. Terapeak enables you to gage that as well as providing other valuable information that you need.

Find a Thirsty Crowd Strategy

For example, you will be able to analyze the top searches and top sellers to determine "what's hot". You can literally make a fortune overnight when you determine "what's hot" because all you would have to do is then find those products that people are thirsty for and desperately want and fulfill that insatiable demand.

I call this strategy "find a thirsty crowd and sell them a drink that will quench their thirst". It's the equivalent of finding a bunch a people in a waterless desert with money in their pockets and you have an endless supply of bottled water to sell to them. Can you imagine the frenzy? They will compete and bid for your water. Something that you paid .50 cent for wholesale would sell for an insane amount of cash.

I give you this analogy because there are products that people would insanely compete and drive the price up on Ebay because the supply is limited. Terapeak allows you to find these types of products.

Here's the strategy that I use employing Terapeak. I make a list of name brand items in five or more distinctive categories. These categories include clothing, shoes, accessories, jewelry, electronics, children toys, sporting goods. Then I come up with specific brand names associated with each category.

For example, if my focus is targeting and making profits from women's, men's and children's clothing I comprised a list of the hottest brand names associated with these particular niches. Here is a detailed list of those brand names that I came up with and used with Terapeak to make money on a consistent and continuous basis.

Women's Apparel Missy

3 Dot
A.B.S
Actionwear
AGB
Alfani
Alfred Dunner
Alice & Olivia
Allen Allen
Anne Klein
August Silk
Bill Blass
Bloomingdale's Now
Briggs
Calvin Klein
Campagne
Carbbean Joe
Chaiken
Charter Club
City DKNY
CLIO
Collection 59
Company By Ellen Tracy
D&G
Dana Buchman
David Dart
Democracy
DkNY
Due-Per-Due
Easy Sprit

Eileen Fisher
Ellen Tracy
Emma James
Fuzzi
French Connection
Gianni
Gloria Vanderbilt
Grace Dane-Lewis
Hot Cotton
INC
Jeanne Pierre
Jennifer Moore
Jessica McClintock
Jones New York
Joseph A.
Karen Kane
Kasper
LaFayette 148
Lauren
Linda Allard
Liz Clairborne
Lucky Brand
M.A.G.
Marc Jacobs
Micheal Kors
Mod-O-Doc
Nine West
Ninety
Norton
Onyx Nites
Ralph Lauren

Reaction
Realities
Sag Harbor
Sage
Sigrid Olsen
Studio M
Style & Co.
Sutton Studion
Tadashi
Tahari
Tamotsu
Tommy Hilfiger
Tractor
Tracy Reece
True Meaning
Tyler
Versage

Women's Contemporary

BCBG
Beautiful People
Bella Dahl
Bisou-Bisou
Cynthia Steffe
Diane Von FurstenBerg
Diesel
Development
Ella Moss

Generra
G-Star
Hard Tail
IISLI
James Perse
Jill Stuart
Joie
Kenneth Cole
Kulson
Language
Laundry
Max Studio
Milly
Miss Sixty
Mint
Nicole Miller
Philip Adec
Punk Royal
Rebecca Taylor
Sanctuary
Shargano
Theory
Triple Five Soul
Tocca
Vince
Warren + White

Women's Junior's

Amy Byer

Aqua
Buffalo
City Triangle
DKNY Jeans
EDC
Energie
Esprit
Eye Shadow
Fang
Free People
Guess
Jet
Jonathan Martin
Juicy Couture
LEI
La Belle
Levi
Lucky Brand
Michael Stars
Mudd
Necessary Objects
Next Era
Paris Blue
Priorities
Puma
Rampage
Roxy
Ruth
Self Esteem
Shameless
Sharagano

So low
To The Max
Tommy Hilfiger
Trixxi
UnionBay
XOXo

Women's Plus Sizes

AGB
Alfani
Allen By Abs
Anne Klein
Bloomingdale's Now
Charter Club
Collection 59
Company By Ellen Tracy
Concept Women
Dan Buchman
David Dart
Democracy
DKNY
DKNY Pure
Due Per Due
Dylan Jeans
Eileen Fisher
Elizabeth
Ellen Tracy
Emma James

Gianni
Gloria Vanderbilt
Hot Cotton
I.N.C.
Jennifer Moore
Karen Kane
Kasper
Lafaette 148
Lauren By Ralph Lauren
Le Suit
Linda Allard
Marina Rinaldi
Rena Rowen
Style & Co.
Sutton Studion
Sweet Pea
Tommy Hilfiger
Tomotsu

Children's Apparel

American Girl
Amy Byer
B.T. Kids
Bonnie Jean
Carter's
Christin Brooks
First Impression
Green Dog

Guess
Jessica McClintock
Jonathan Martin
La Belle
Miken Kids
Mudd
My Michelle
Oshkosh B Gosh
OTB Jeanswear
QuickSilver
Ralph Lauren
Roxy
Sean John
Speechless
Tommy Hilfiger

Men's Apparel

Alfani
American Rag
BC Ethic
Bill Blass
Brandini
Calvin Klein
Charter Club
ClaiBorne
Club Room
DKNY
Dockers

Ecko UNLTD.
Evan Picone
Exte
Extreme Gear
Geoffrey Beene
G-Star
Guess
Hurley
INC
IZOD
Jones NY
Joeseph & Lyman
Kenneth Cole
Levi
Metropolitan View
Micheal Kors
Nautica
Naturalife
Oscar De La Renta
Perry Ellis
Plugg
Polo Sport
QuickSilver
Ralph Lauren
Reunion
Savane
Split
Tommy Hilfiger
Tasso Elba
UnionBay

Micro Targeting

Now that I had a list of hot brand names, I use the strategy of micro targeting. What exactly is micro targeting? Micro targeting is instead of trying to sell to the whole universe of people in the Ebay marketplace that are interested in a particular designer brand name like for example BCBG, I targeted an even more specific niche, women who are looking for BCBG Cocktail dresses.

I use this particular strategy because I believe in finding a lucrative niche and dominating it. So now that I knew who and what I am targeting, it was time to use the Ebay's Marketplace research tool (now known as Terapeak) to see if there was a lucrative market for women seeking BCBG cocktail dresses.

So I typed in the keywords BCBG cocktail dress and I clicked on the drop down arrow in the category menu and chose the category clothing shoes and accessories and I then proceeded to click on women's clothing to refine my search. Then I clicked on the completed items tab and chose a time period in which to analyze. I chose to analyze all the results of the auctions of this style of dresses that occurred in the last month.

I clicked on the run research button and these were the results. Marketplace research showed that there were a total of 5,622 completed items and out of these completed items 3,800 items sold. That was a whopping 67%. I knew instantly from these results that this was indeed a lucrative market.

My definition of lucrative is the ability to sell an item for a substantial profit as well as getting repeat sales from the same customers for a similar item. Of course, that item as it relates to cocktail dresses would have to be a different style or color to get repeat sales.

Remember that I previously mentioned the "find a thirsty crowd and sell them a drink that will quench their thirst" strategy? Well getting repeat sales from the same customers is the equivalent of selling that same thirsty crowd who's thirst you have previously quench a second drink. The **second drink strategy** works phenomenally well when you have a well stocked Ebay store because your customers have a place that they can always come back to make additional purchases.

Speaking on the subject of Ebay stores if you decide that you want to dominate different niche markets I suggest that you have additional Ebay usernames and stores. By the way you are allowed to have multiple accounts on Ebay and you should take advantage of this rule.

Here's why. If you are selling clothing in your Ebay store it is best to have in your store inventory nothing but clothing items and accessories items because you want to convey to the buyer that you are a specialist in this category. It's the psychology of selling and buying.

I mean can you imagine if you had 1,000 other products in your Ebay store in addition to the clothing you are selling like toys, electronics, cars, and other knick knacks? The potential buyer not only would have to navigate through this maze of various products but they will also get distracted.

So if you want to sell additional specialized products like electronics for example just create another Ebay store designed specifically for electronics products. If you're having trouble grasping this concept the logic is simply this, would you go to a Pizza shop to get your car fixed?

Ok now that you found out the vital statistics, it is time to locate the wholesale suppliers of that product. Your goal of course would be to find the suppliers that are selling the product for a much lower price for what it is selling for on Ebay. While on the subject of suppliers let's discuss the various ways in which you can buy from them.

First of all there are a spectrum of suppliers. On one end of the spectrum you have liquidation, close-outs, shelf pulls, and the overstock market. The prices are great. You can actually get products for 5 to 10 cents on the dollar. They might not be the most current or latest model, but that doesn't necessarily matter. Your risk however is much higher. So on one end we have low prices, high risk.

At the other end of the spectrum there are dropshippers. With dropshippers you have minimal risk but sometimes getting a decent profit spread can be a challenge if you are doing it in a conventional way. Don't get me wrong I make a ton of cash using dropshipping but like everything else you have to locate the right suppliers who have the right products at the right price.

In between the spectrum you have wholesalers. There are light bulk wholesalers where you can spend $500 or less. Then there are Bulk wholesalers that require a larger cash outlay. In my money making Ebay blue print, I personally use a combination of all the aforementioned suppliers to generate a ton of cash on Ebay.

For example, getting back to our clothing example I use a company called DLM Off Price Specialist out in California. This place is an absolute goldmine and I have made a fortune on Ebay using them. They sell high end designer brand clothing, shoes and accessories at a fraction of their cost. They buy their items from high end stores like Bloomingdales when they have overstock and store returns. These are first quality authentic items that come with the store tags.

When it comes to women items they sell these items for only 17% of the actual retail price. So those BCBG Cocktail dresses you can get them at a fraction of the cost. For example, I bought 10 of these styles of dresses recently and this what I paid for them.

BCBG Dress #1 had a retail price of $425 and I paid only 17% of that retail price which amounted to $72.00.

BCBG Dress #2 had a retail price of $319 and I paid only 17% of that retail price which amounted to $54.23.

BCBG Dress #3 had a retail price of $305 and I paid only 17% of that retail price which amounted to $51.85.

BCBG Dress #4 had a retail price of $297 and I paid only 17% of that retail price which amounted to $50.49.

BCBG Dress #5 had a retail price of $217 and I paid only 17% of that retail price which amounted to $36.89.

BCBG Dress #6 had a retail price of $219 and I paid only 17% of that retail price which amounted to $37.23.

BCBG Dress #7 had a retail price of $227 and I paid only 17% of that retail price which amounted to $38.59.

BCBG Dress #8 had a retail price of $117 and I paid only 17% of that retail price which amounted to $19.89.

BCBG Dress #9 had a retail price of $122 and I paid only 17% of that retail price which amounted to $20.74.

BCBG Dress #10 had a retail price of $147 and I paid only 17% of that retail price which amounted to $24.99.

I know that you are probably saying to yourself those are some incredible prices to buy those items at! I agree and what's even more incredible were the profits I made from them. Let's tally the numbers up. I paid an insanely low price of $406.90 for 10 BCBG cocktail dresses with a retail value of $2,395. So I actually had a potential gross profit of $1,988.10 if Ebay buyers paid full retail value for these dresses. The great thing is these dresses were hot, in style and in demand.

Of course I wasn't going to list them for the retail value because Ebay buyers come to Ebay to look for deals. The strategy that I used was I marked up each and every dress 3 times higher for what I paid for them. Here's the break down.

Dress #1 which I paid $72 for I started the opening bid price at $216 which was $209 below the actual retail price.

Dress #2 which I paid $54.23 for I started the opening bid price at $162.69 which was $142.31 below the actual retail price.

Dress #3 which I paid $51.85 for I started the opening bid price at $155.55 which was $149.95 below the actual retail price.

Dress #4 which I paid $50.49 for I started the opening bid price at $151.47 which was $145.53 below the actual retail price.

Dress #5 which I paid $36.89 for I started the opening bid price at $110.67 which was $106.33 below the actual retail price.

Dress #6 which I paid $37.23 for I started the opening bid price at $111.69 which was $107.31 below the actual retail price.

Dress #7 which I paid $38.59 for I started the opening bid price at $115.77 which was $103.23 below the actual retail price.

Dress #8 which I paid $19.89 for I started the opening bid price at $59.67 which was $57.33 below the actual retail price.

Dress #9 which I paid $20.74 for I started the opening bid price at $62.22 which was $59.78 below the actual retail price.

Dress #10 which I paid $24.99 for I started the opening bid price at $74.97 which was $72.03 below the actual retail price.

Here are the results of those 10 auctions that I listed.

Dress #1 sold for $283.27 my gross profit was $211.27($283.27-$72.00=$211.27)

Dress #2 sold for $172.20 my gross profit $117.97($172.20-$54.23=$117.97

Dress #3 sold for $272.22 which was close to the actual retail price of $305 my gross profit was $220.37. ($272.22-$51.85=$220.37)

Dress #4 didn't sell initially so I had to relist it again. The second time around it sold for $151.47. My gross profit was $100.98($151.47-$50.49=$100.98)

Dress #5 sold for $183.19 which was close to the actual retail price of $217 my gross profit was $146.30. ($183.19-$36.89=$146.30)

Dress #6 sold for $137.90 my gross profit was $100.67($137.90-$37.23=$100.67)

Dress #7 sold for $140.00 my gross profit was $101.41($140.00-$38.59=$101.41)

Dress #8 sold for the $59.67 I started the opening bid at. My gross profit was $39.78($59.67-$19.89=$39.78)

Dress #9 sold for $101.00. My gross profit was $80.26($101.00-$20.74=$80.26)

Dress #10 sold for the $74.97 I started the opening bid at. My gross profit was $49.98($74.97-$24.99=$49.98)

Gross Profit Versus Net Profit

I intentionally gave you what I grossed for the sale of each of the 10 dresses versus giving you the net profit because I want you to realize that it is truly about the net profit which is simply what you get to keep. So when I talk about you making $10,000 or more a month on Ebay I'm talking about the net profit.

A lot of Ebay sellers appear to be making a lot of money on Ebay and a lot of them are but most of them make very little money after all their expenses are deducted from their gross profit. Their problem is this they don't know how to buy items for resale. They buy items that offer very little markup and the profit margins are thin.

For example, let's say you bought an item at a so called "wholesale price" of $79 and the average price this item is selling on Ebay for is $99. You decide to list it in a fixed price auction with a price of $99 because you know what you need to sell it at in order for you to make a profit.

In addition, the Ebay marketplace indicates that $99 is the most they are willing to pay for this item. Your listing or insertion fee that Ebay will charge you is $2.40. If you include a picture in your auction and you should, the first one is free of charge and .15 cent per picture thereafter. Let's say you decide to only include one picture in your auction for this example.

Ebay has a gallery picture feature which allows you to show a picture of your item to potential buyers without them having to click on the actual link that leads them to your listing. The cost to include a picture in the gallery is .35 and I would say that it is a must for you to use this feature to attract potential buyers.

So let's add up the expenses so far. Listing fees $2.40, Gallery picture .35 cent, "wholesale price" of the item $79, and cost to ship the item to you $6.20. So far your expenses total $8.95. So let's say that you actually sold that item on the first go around for $99. Once you have sold the item there are additional fees. Ebay charges you a final valuation fee of $3.07. This fee is nothing more than their cut for allowing you to sell your item on Ebay.

But wait, that's not all that they charge. Ebay owns Paypal so they also make money from you when someone sends their payment to you through Paypal. This is what Paypal is going to charge you. Although you will be passing on the shipping charges to your customer, Paypal is still going to charge you based on the total amount of money that the customer has sent for payment.

So if you sold your item to the customer at $99 plus you charged a shipping and handling fee of $6.20, Paypal is going to charged you based on the total payment which is $105.20. The fee that they will charge you to receive this payment is $3.35. Paypal calculates this fee the following way. They charge 2.9% of the $105.20 which amounts to $3.05 plus they charge an additional .30 cents for the transaction. So that brings your total Paypal fees to $3.35.

Now let's add up all the expenses and deduct it from the gross profit to get to the net profit. Total expenses $94.37 which includes the $79 you paid for the item plus $2.40 listing fee plus .35 cent gallery picture plus $6.20 shipping charge to ship item to you plus $3.07 final valuation fee and the Paypal fees totaling $3.35.Now deduct the total expenses of $94.37 from your gross which totals $99 your NET PROFIT is only $4.63.

Sadly a lot of Ebay sellers who don't know the fundamentals of business sell on Ebay this way and claim that they are "making money". Furthermore, the previous example was based on the fact that you sold your item on the first go around. But what if you didn't sell the item the first time around and had to relist it again. Ok if you had to do that Ebay doesn't charge you to relist if you list it a second time and it sold.

But what if you didn't sell it after you listed a second time and you decided to list it a third time, Ebay charges you another listing fee regardless of whether you sold it or not. So your profit margin dwindles an additional $2.40 the listing fee). If you have to relist again after that you actually have almost zero profit margin.

Bullet Proof Strategy

You don't want to ever experience a zero profit margin because you will be just wasting your time as well as your money. That's why I usually sell an item for at least 2 times higher or more for what I have paid for it. This ensures that if it doesn't sell the first time around or even the second or third time around I could relist it without the danger of selling it for breakeven, no profit at all or even at a loss.

That's why my strategy with the dresses was to buy them significantly below wholesale prices and then starting my auctions off with a initial opening bid price of 3 times of what I paid for them. I call this my bullet proof profit strategy.

So always remember this golden rule. To ensure healthy net profits for yourself you must calculate the cost associated with doing business on Ebay. That includes what you actually paid for the product, the listing fees, the relisting fees, the final valuation fees, the Paypal fees, the shipping fees, etc.

My Total Net Profit From Selling 10 BCBG Cocktail Dresses

Dress #1
Sale Price of Dress 283.27
Cost of dress   (72.00)
Insertion fee   (3.60)
Gallery fee   (.35)
final valuation fee (9.70)
paypal fees   (8.86)
==============================

Net Profit   = $188.76

Dress #2
Sale Price of Dress 172.20
Cost of dress   (54.23)
Insertion fee   (2.40)
Gallery fee   (.35)
final valuation fee   (6.09)
paypal fees   (5.64)
==============================

Net Profit   = $103.49

Dress #3
Sale Price of Dress 272.22
Cost of dress   (51.85)
Insertion fee   (2.40)
Gallery fee   (.35)
final valuation fee   (9.34)
paypal fees   (8.54)
==============================

Net Profit   = $199.74

Dress #4
Sale Price of Dress 151.47
Cost of dress   (50.49)

Insertion fee   (2.40)
Gallery fee   (.35)
final valuation fee (5.42)
paypal fees   (5.04)
===============================
Net Profit   = $87.77

Dress #5
Sale Price of Dress 183.19
Cost of dress   (36.89)
Insertion fee   (2.40)
Gallery fee   (.35)
final valuation fee (6.45)
paypal fees   (5.96)
===============================
Net Profit   = $131.14

Dress #6
Sale Price of Dress 137.90
Cost of dress   (37.23)
Insertion fee   (2.40)
Gallery fee   (.35)
final valuation fee (4.98)
paypal fees   (4.65)
===============================
Net Profit   = $88.29

Dress #7
Sale Price of Dress 140.00
Cost of dress   (38.59)
Insertion fee   (2.40)
Gallery fee   (.35)
final valuation fee (5.05)
paypal fees   (4.71)
===============================
Net Profit   = $88.90

Dress #8

Sale Price of Dress 59.67
Cost of dress   (19.89)
Insertion fee   (2.40)
Gallery fee   (.35)
final valuation fee (2.44)
paypal fees   (2.38)
============================

Net Profit   = $32.21

Dress #9
Sale Price of Dress 101.00
Cost of dress   (20.74)
Insertion fee   (2.40)
Gallery fee   (.35)
final valuation fee (3.57)
paypal fees   (3.58)
============================

Net Profit   = $70.36

Dress #10
Sale Price of Dress 74.97
Cost of dress   (24.99)
Insertion fee   (2.40)
Gallery fee   (.35)
final valuation fee (2.93)
paypal fee   (2.82)
============================

Net Profit   = $41.48

My total net profit from the sale of the 10 dresses was $1012.14 after I deducted the $20 DLM charged me for the shipment of the dresses.

After I successfully sold those 10 dresses I decided to invest in more BCBG dresses as well as other well known hot designer brands like Nicole Miller, Eileen Fisher, Dana Buchman and others. I went for the kill and loaded up my Ebay store up with these fast moving women items.

I consistently made $10,000 or more in net profit every thirty days. So if it is your desire and goal to make $10,000 or more a month on Ebay you should consider selling high end designer brand name clothing and accessories.

Of course as with any investment, you must do your research and due diligence before you invest your capital. Before I continue on let me give you DLM's contact information as well as other off price clothing specialists and closeout companies that offer great deals on women's, men's and children's clothing items.

List of Off Price Clothing Specialists and Closeout Companies

DLM Off Price Specialist
2343 Saybrook Ave
Commerce, California 90040
Tel # (323)724-5474

http://www.dlmoffprice.com

E-Fashion Wholesale
3352 9South Freehold, New Jersey 07728
(732) 866-9976
http://www.efashionwholesale.com

J & P Sales Incorporated
4901 Patata Street Unit 201
Cudahy, California 90201
 (323) 560-1210
http://www.jnpsales.com

Madison Avenue Closeouts
5400 West WT Harris Blvd Suite K
Charlotte, North Carolina 28269
(866) 795-7990
http://www.madisonavenuecloseouts.com

Ben Elias
1400 Broadway 29th Floor
New York, New York 10018
(212) 354-8300
 http://www.benelias.com

BG International
13144 Old West Ave
San Diego, California 92190
 (858) 538-8670
 http://www.bg-intl.com

CMD Wholesale
3501 Silver Side Road

87

Wilmington, Delaware 19810
 (877) 263-9695
http://www.cmdwholesale.com

Fashion Depot
46 Fourth Ave
Long Branch, New Jersey 07740
(877) 229-4469
 http://www.thefashiondepot.com

Merchandise Outlet
8956 Sorensen Ave. Suite 8
Santa Fe Springs, California 90670
 http://www.merchandise-outlet.com

Atlantic Surplus
3224 N. College Rd. Suite 169
Wilmington, North Carolina 28405
(910) 798-8075
 http://www.alanticsurplus.com

Once again these are quality legitimate companies that sell authentic brand name merchandise at wholesale and even below wholesale prices. If you utilize these ten companies I've just mentioned and do your research, you will dominate the name brand clothing niche on Ebay and make a ton of money.

How To Crush The Competition Using the "Karate Chop Strategy"

When you sell on Ebay make no mistakes about it you will be facing some competition. In fact, in most cases the competition will be stiff if you are selling products that have a strong demand.

During Ebay's infancy you mostly had Mom and Pop operations and average Joe's and Jane's selling products and stuff that they had in their basements and attics. Well that's not the case any longer. You now have mid-size to large businesses now hawking their goods on Ebay.

So how do you compete with them as well as with other sellers who are selling similar items to yours? The answer is by using what I refer to as "the karate chop strategy". The karate chop strategy entails adding a unique and complimentary item to your already existing auctions.

This will not only enhance your auctions but it will distinguish them and separate you from the crowd of sellers because you will be the only doing it. That's why the complimentary item must be unique. If it is unique you instantly and uniquely position yourself in the Ebay marketplace.

For example, I began to encounter stiff competition selling designer dresses. I mean some sellers were actually selling them for a lower price but what I did to thwart this was I added jewelry to go along with the dresses.

This enabled me to change the perception value wise of the dresses that I was selling because I wasn't just selling high end designer dresses like everyone else but now I was selling "elegance" when I added the jewelry which consisted of diamond and gold rings, necklaces and bracelets. I uniquely positioned myself in the crowded marketplace and won. The margins on the jewelry were great! Here's is the strategy that I used to purchase the jewelry.

I purchased my jewelry at two places, one was http://www.bidz.com and the other one was Midtown Closeout Jewelry Warehouse. Bidz.com is actually an auction place similar to Ebay. It is the largest interactive online jewelry auction where you can get jewelry at incredible prices. Auctions at Bidz start off at $1 every five seconds and their live auctions run 24 hours a day and 7 days a week.

Midtown Closeout Jewelry Warehouse is the World's largest below wholesale liquidator of fine jewelry closeouts. You can get any piece of jewelry under the sun. Here is an example of how I used Bidz to "karate chop" the competition.

My unique selling position as I said before with my designer dress auctions was to convey and sell "elegance" so I bid on and won jewelry items at Bidz.com that was the epitome of "elegance". For example, I won a bid on a pair of irresistible pair of genuine sapphire earrings that had 1.26 ctw diamonds and made of 18k solid yellow gold I won the bid and paid only $158 for a pair of earrings that had a retail value of $1700.

These fabulous earrings had SI1-SI2 eye clean clarity. On Bidz you can request a gemological report for that item that you won. This report provides reliable details such as the identification, authentication, content and weight of the gems or precious metals contained in an item.

In addition the report also includes an enlarged color photograph which shows further identifying information. All gemological analysis are done by a highly qualified independent gemological laboratory.

As part of my marketing strategy because I know that people are inherently skeptical I stated in the description of my auction that the winning bidder would get this official report that verified and backed up my claims. I even offered a double your money back guarantee to them if they had another official appraisal done and it was proved that my claims proved to be false.

So remember to offer strong guarantees because when you 100% guarantee something you are practicing the concept of risk reversal. You eliminate the risk from the customer and transfer it to yourself. The stronger the guarantee the more likely you will make the sale.

I combined these fabulous earrings with a 100% silk BCBG cocktail dress that retailed for $192 and I paid only $32.64. Once again I marked the dress up 3X what I paid for it which amounted to $97.92. I decided to give the potential buyer the earrings for 75% off the actual retail price of $1700 which amounted to $425. A 3X times markup of what I paid for them.

My goal was to craft an irresistible offer that would entice potential bidders to compete on the auction. I started the opening bid at $522.92 and that's what it sold for. My total Ebay fees were $22.29 this included the listing fee and the final valuation fee. My Paypal fees were $15.81 to collect a total payment of $534.92 from the customer. $12 of this total amount consisted of the shipping charge.

My net profit from this one auction was $294.18. I effectively sold "elegance" and karate chopped the competition who were only selling designer dresses. Let's take a look at the numbers. If you did this 34 times within a 30 day period you would make $10,000. It's that simple. It's all about executing the strategy and adjusting it when you have to.

I saw that the field was getting really competitive and I adjusted like a quarterback does when all of sudden he realizes that he is being blitzed. Not only was I unique in my approach in thwarting the competition, but also as a result of having a keyword like diamond earrings in the auction title it attracted bidders who were strictly looking for diamond earrings and saw the designer dress as a delightful bonus.

"The Karate Chop" strategy works with any item that you intend to sell on Ebay, you just have to remember that the additional item that you include in your auction should uniquely distinguish you from the competition.

Once again if you want to purchase great women's and men's jewelry at way below wholesale prices at Bidz simply visit the following web address http://www.bidz.com and register with them. Midtown Closeout Jewelry Warehouse is another phenomenal place that you can use. Their only requirement is that you have to purchase $300 worth of items. You can access them by visiting the following web address http://www.midtowncloseout.com. Here are some other great places to buy jewelry and watches wholesale.

Great Places To Buy Jewelry and Wholesale Watches

Sid Birzon Inc.
1376 Niagara Falls Blvd
Tonawanda, New York 14150
Toll-Free: 800-783-8250
http://www.wholesalecentral.com/sidbirzon

Wholesale Wholesale
1015 Gayley Ave. Suite 600
Los Angeles, California 90024
(800) 519-3221
http://www.wholesalewholesale.com

Zach Trading Company
4428 Pembroke Rd Hollywood, Florida 33021
 (800) 777-7767
 http://www.zacktrading.com

Liquidation.com
http://www.liquidation.com

#1 Accesorios
1700 N Solano Drive LAS CRUCES, NM 88001
(505) 350-9907
http://www.1accesorios.com

Sylvia Sterling Jewelry Design
72 Wood Lane Fairfax CA 94930
(415)460-1089
http://www.sylviajewelry.com

New City Inc Wholesale Watch Sellers
21 SE 1st Avenue
Miami, Florida 33131
(305) 371-4188
 http://www.newcityinc.com

Windsor Wholesale Jewelry
111 Flagship Drive Lutz, Florida 33549
 (813) 909-4832
http://www.windsorwholesalejewelry.com

National Diamond and Gold
410 Burr Oak
Tip City, Ohio 45371

(937) 667-9514
http://www.national-diamond-gold.com

Jewelry Sprite
9990 SW 77th Ave. Penthouse 18
Miami, Florida 33516
(800) 635-0548
http://www.jewelrysprite.com

In total I've given you 12 jewelry companies that
you can use in a variety of ways to make a ton of
money on Ebay.

"It's used but so what strategy"

Before I reveal to you the places where you can buy
new electronic items via wholesale and dropshipping, I
want to first enlighten you to a very potent strategy that
you can use to jumpstart your profits on Ebay. It's a
strategy that I consistently utilize and I refer to it as the
"It's used but so what strategy". This strategy entails
selling used items on Ebay.

The majority of the people whom desire it is to
make money as sellers on Ebay approach this goal with
a conventional mindset. That mindset is to buy new
products wholesale, mark them up and sell them for a
profit on Ebay. You see the problem with this strategy
sometimes is the majority of Ebay sellers are using this
same approach which leads to people selling similar
products in an overcrowded market place and as a

result the profit margins are slim because of the fierce competition.

For example, I wanted to sell Global Positioning Systems or GPS devices on Ebay because I knew there was a strong demand for them. However, the wholesale suppliers were selling them at a price where it would be impossible for me to make a profit on Ebay. So what did I do? I employed the "It's used but so what strategy". I simply bought used GPS systems and resold them on Ebay. Where did I get these used GPS from? Believe or not on Ebay and a place called Craig's List.

You have to understand the mentality of people who are selling something that they don't want and they no longer have any use for. They are more apt to negotiate with you especially in the case of used items. Craig's list is nothing like Ebay. There is no auction listing with bidding, so there is a lot of room for negotiation for items for sale and the great thing is you're not restricted and forced to adhere to ridiculous rules like you are on Ebay regarding the sale of items.

After, doing my research using marketplace research I discovered that there was a high demand for Garmin Nuvi 350 global positioning systems. The average price it was going for on Ebay was $375 in new condition. I capitalized on this demand by buying them used on Craig's List. For example, one seller posted for sale a used but in great condition Garmin Nuvi 350 GPS.

He said he had it for 6 months and he stated the reason why he was selling it because he just bought a GPS with the latest features. He wanted $270 for it but of course I wasn't trying to pay that price for it. I met up with him and that's the great thing about Craig's list it is local and you will be primarily dealing with people in your area and I offered him $160 for it on the spot.

He hemmed and hawed but when I said the following line to him he conceded to this price. "So you're saying if I don't pay you $270 that means we can't do business today?" He replied "I'm not saying that......" and I quickly interjected and said "Ok so here's the $160" and he accepted it. This is known as the "takeaway close." To tell you the truth I think that he only conceded to the price of $160 because I was probably his only option at the time.

Nonetheless, I listed the used GPS on Ebay and sold it for $265 netting a profit of $105. As you can clearly see using the "it's used but so what" strategy can pay big dividends for you. You just have to remember to not always follow the tide of what other sellers are doing. A lot of money can be made selling on Ebay in an unconventional way.

Staying on the subject of approaching selling and buying in unconventional ways, you can actually buy items from Ebay at wholesale prices and below wholesale price and resell them. As I mentioned previously you have midsize to large businesses also hawking items on Ebay at dirt cheap prices. You also have wholesale companies selling their inventory to the public using Ebay.

How do you actually find these wholesale items for sale? You just simply type the word wholesale or the word lot after the item's name that you are looking for. For example, if you're looking for digital cameras, you would type the following search term in Ebay's search engine: digital cameras wholesale or digital cameras lot or you can include both search terms digital cameras wholesale lot. Your search will return items from sellers selling digital cameras wholesale and in lots. I bought used Global Positioning Systems (GPS) using this keyword search strategy.

I also used this strategy to buy the popular and in demand Blackberry PDA cell phones. These Blackberry PDA phones were mainly used but it didn't matter to Ebayer's who were in search of them at bargain prices. In fact, I purchased five of these Rim Blackberry 7290 cellular phones on Ebay for $170 and resold them on Ebay individually a week later tripling my money.

Can you make $10,000 or more in 30 days buying items on Ebay in lots or wholesale? You sure can because I have done it.

Buying items from a company called liquidation.com is another great way to find items at dirt cheap prices for resale on Ebay. At Liquidation.com buyers can source commercial surplus inventory and government surplus assets in an online environment. Bulk lots are sold by the truckload, pallet, or small package, and conditions range from new in a box to customer returns and used. They have a wide variety of product categories that includes apparel, computers, electronics, housewares, industrial equipment, vehicles, and much more. You can access them by visiting the following web address on the internet. http://www.liquidation.com

"The Refurb Strategy"

What is "the refurb strategy"? "The refurb strategy" is simply selling factory refurbished products on Ebay for tremendous profits. So why are products labeled refurbished? Here are some examples:

- Most major retail superstores offer a 30-day money back guarantee on their products and there are those consumers that just simply take advantage of that. These items are returned to the manufacturer, inspected and repackaged like new.

- Items where the box or casing was damaged in shipment which are returned to the manufacturer.

- Item was returned to the manufacturer because of a slight defect. The part that was defective was replaced by the manufacturer, tested and then repackaged just like new.

- The item was returned because of a minor cosmetic blemish on the casing that was corrected.

- Demonstration units are also considered factory refurbished. These units are inspected, tested and repackaged.

- The box was simply opened.

- Brand new overstocked items are also labeled factory refurbished.

When you buy factory refurbished products you get them at tremendously low prices which allows you to make money on Ebay reselling them. A word of caution, when you are listing refurbished products on Ebay you must fully disclosed the fact that they are refurbished to avoid potential problems you may have with buyers.

I'm going to give you two companies that offer tremendous deals for refurbished electronic items. These are my secrets sources that I am revealing so handle with care!

Refurbished Electronics Companies

Refurbish Depot
1449 37th Street
Brooklyn, New York 11218
(718) 686-7445 http://www.refurbdepot.com

FactoryDirectDeals.com
7171 N Davis Highway Pensacola, Florida 32504
 (850) 777-8787

http://www.factorydirectdeals.com

Companies that Sell New Electronic Items

Ok as promised now I am going to give the companies that sell new electronic items.

Thunderball Marketing
10 Cragwood Road Avenel, New Jersey 07001
 (732) 388-5000
 http://www.tball.com

A to Z Micro-Technologies Inc.
3700 Golf Colont Lane
Little River, South Carolina 29566
(631)517-9179
 http://www.atozonline.com

CWR Electronics
245-1 Hickory Lane Bayville, New Jersey 08721
 (732) 237-9300
 http://www.cwrelectronics.com

Price Master Corporation
57-07 31st Ave.
Woodside, New York 11377
 (800) 538-3873
 http://www.pricemaster.com

Premier Products International
6402 Badger Drive Tampa, FL 33610
 (813)621-6673

http://www.hotbuy4u.com

"Big Profit Strategy"

The "Big Profit Strategy" entails concentrating only on items that will bring you a minimum profit margin of $500 and above. Why sell a ton of items with small margins to make $10,000 or more a month when you can easily sell a few items with higher margins with a lot less effort?

For example, if your average profit margin per item is $40 you would have to sell 250 of these items to make $10,000. If the average profit margin was $25 you would have to sell 400 items. I don't know about you but I would rather sell 10 items that had a profit margin of $1,000 per item to make $10,000 rather than 400 items because it is a lot easier to sell 10 of something that is in demand versus 400 of something that is in demand.

Ideally, it would be even better to have to sell only 1 item with a profit margin of $10,000 to make $10,000. Make Sense? Of course it does and that's why I am a big proponent of the "Big Profit Strategy" because it requires you to think big profits rather than small profits and plus I would rather work less and make more anyway.

So how do you make a minimum of $500 or more on an item on Ebay? You would simply focus on Big

Ticket Items. I know that you are probably saying "I can't afford to sell big ticket items" and to that I simply say bull crap. You need to start thinking outside of the box. You don't necessarily have to own or buy these big ticket items to do business on Ebay. You can use what I refer to as "the Option strategy".

The Option Strategy

The option strategy entails entering into a contractual agreement with the owner of the big ticket item I mentioned previously that states that you have the right to buy that item at a specific price by a certain date.

For example, let's say that a local used car dealer in your city or town was trying to sell a particular used car for $8,000 to no avail. You approached this used car dealer and offered them your assistance to sell the car if they gave you an exclusive option to buy it for $6,000 in 7 days.

Once this agreement is signed by both parties on the dotted line you then would list that used car on Ebay motors in a 5 day auction and you would set your opening bid price at $8,000. The cost to list this used car on Ebay motors is a $40 insertion fee and a $50 transaction service fee when you receive the first bid on it. There are no additional fees charged after you have sold the car. The car sells at that $8,000 price. Your gross profit would be $2,000. Your net would be just a little bit less than the $2,000 when you deduct the Ebay fees and other incidental expenses that maybe associated with selling the car.

But what if you don't sell the car? The only thing you are out of is the $40 insertion fee because your agreement with the used car dealer would contain a provision that if you decide not to buy that vehicle in the 7 day time period the contract is automatically voided. Pretty creative huh? This is nothing more than "thinking outside of the box".

You can apply the option strategy with any big ticket item. However, I suggest that you consult with an attorney and have them draw up a simple option agreement that spells out the terms between you and the owner.

Okay there you have it, the secrets as well as the strategies to make $10,000 or more on Ebay in 30 days. As you can clearly see, this is not a get rich quick scheme. It is a thorough plan that requires continuous research, flexibility and refinement of selling strategies in order to reach that ultimate goal of making $10,000 or more on Ebay in 30 days. I say "or more" because there are no limits to what you can actually make. However, the amount you make depends entirely on you. Think and plan big and you will be successful!

Other Books Written By Omar Johnson

Search Engine Domination: "The Ultimate Secrets To Increasing Your Website's Visibility And Making a Ton of Cash"

How To Sell Any Product Online: "Secrets of The Killer Sales Letter"

How To Make Money Online: "The Savvy Entrepreneur's Guide to Financial Freedom"

How To Create A Profitable Ezine From Scratch

The Secrets of Finding The Perfect Ghostwriter For Your Book

How To Overcome Your Self-Limiting Beliefs & Achieve Anything You Want

Creative Real Estate Investing Strategies and Tips

How To Make A Fortune Using The Public Domain

The Complete Guide To Investing In Gold And Silver: Surviving The Great Economic Depression

How To Promote Market And Sell Your Kindle Book

How To Start An Online Business With Less Than $200

The Creative Real Estate Marketing Equation: Motivated Sellers + Motivated Buyers = $

How To Market Your Business Online And Offline